Waxing for Skiers

Malcolm Corcoran

STACKPOLE BOOKS

0 11557 03126 3

Copyright © 1999 by Stackpole Books

First published in Canada in 1997 by Guy Saint-Jean Editeur Inc.
Translated from French by Dave Martin

Published by
STACKPOLE BOOKS
5067 Ritter Road
Mechanicsburg, PA 17055
www.stackpolebooks.com

Printed in United States

First edition

10 9 8 7 6 5 4 3 2 1

Cover design by Wendy Reynolds

Cover photo by Effin Older

Library of Congress Cataloging-in-Publication Data
Corcoran, Malcolm, 1948—
 Waxing for skiers / Malcolm Corcoran.
  p. cm.
 ISBN 0-8117-3126-X (pbk.)
 1. Ski waxing. 2. Skis and skiing—Equipment and supplies—
 Maintenance and repair. I. Title.
GV855.5.W39C67   1999   99-33962
796.93—dc21   CIP

TABLE OF CONTENTS

FOREWORD

Cross-country skiing is an integral part of my life. It is a discipline that provides never-ending challenges and pleasures. While training and competing in biathlons, which combine cross-country skiing and rifle shooting, I've traveled many kilometers on snow-covered trails. There I fully realized the importance of waxing cross-country skis.

Correct waxing has proved to be a determining factor for me; it has helped me win medals at several international competitions and even at the Olympic Games. Not everyone aspires to qualify for international competitions. Nonetheless, obtaining maximum ski performance in diverse conditions through effective waxing is a challenge that faces every skier.

This book is a clear, well organized presentation of all the most frequently used ski-waxing operations and techniques. It describes waxing as a combination of knowledge and skills that are easy to learn and master.

Whether you are a novice or an advanced skier, learning the art of waxing will help you enjoy this marvelous sport even more.

Myriam Bédard
Gold medalist at the
Lillehammer, Norway,
Olympic Games in 1994

ACKNOWLEDGMENTS

I would like to thank Pierre Harvey, former North American and World Cup cross country champion, and Myriam Bédard, gold medalist at the Lillehammer (Norway) Olympics and World Cup biathlon champion, for their support and collaboration.

Special thanks to Pierre Langevin of Swix Canada and Bernard Voyer of Biathlon Canada, who shared with me their vast knowledge of waxing and whose advice was indispensable. I would also like to thank Ross Corcoran and Francine André for the illustrations and Éric Corcoran for being available and providing support. I would be remiss if I did not acknowledge the patient and painstaking revision of this text by my wife, Lise.

INTRODUCTION

Cross-country skiing has become a very popular sport in recent years. To appreciate it fully, however, skiers must wax their skis correctly. Skiers who can take a diagonal stride or use the skating technique to climb or go quickly down hills enjoy the sport more and derive greater satisfaction from it. Choosing the right wax and applying it correctly to properly prepared skis can make the difference between an enjoyable run and a disastrous one.

Waxing is a simple and interesting operation, but as with any skill, you must know what to do and how to do it. This book explains what different types of waxes do, outlines the sequence in which they are to be applied, and describes various application techniques. It also explains how to select the wax for a particular day, and provides waxing tables and advice on waxing equipment. Skiers of all levels from novice to expert will be able to experiment with and adapt this information to develop strategies and skills that suit their needs.

Portions of this book also apply to downhill skis and snowboards. The same waxes and waxing techniques are appropriate, because the bases of the skis and snowboards are made of the same materials.

GENERAL PRECAUTIONS

- Some waxes or additives used in very cold temperatures crumble when they are cold-scraped. Wear goggles. Remove excess wax while it is still hot and go over it a second time when it has cooled off.
- Noxious gases may be produced during the application of fluorocarbon waxes. Wear a mask and work only in a well-ventilated room when using such waxes or when using wax remover.
- Wear vinyl gloves and avoid skin contact with wax remover or any toxic material used in the waxing process. Wear gloves for pine tar and binder wax applications.
- To avoid burning waxes completely and producing toxic gas emissions, do not heat fluorocarbon glider waxes to temperatures exceeding 570° F (300° C).
- Do not smoke in a room where skis are being waxed.
- Dispose of wax remover-soaked cloths immediately.
- Keep containers of wax remover away from sources of intense heat such as waxing irons and torches.
- Turn off torch valves tightly after use.

1

The Basics

WAXING DEFINED

Waxing involves preparing the bases of skis and applying wax to improve their performance. Proper waxing enables you to push forward without backsliding and glide quickly when skiing in the classic style. It also helps freestyle skiers glide quickly and easily. Wax protects the bases from shocks and scratches while the skis are in use, in transit, or in storage, and it prevents the bases from deteriorating. Proper waxing makes it easier to learn skiing techniques, which in turn can help you to save energy, ski more safely, and enjoy more satisfying and pleasant cross-country ski outings.

How you wax your skis depends on the skiing style, the type of ski, the ski base material, and the types of wax you select.

SKI STYLES

There are two primary cross-country skiing styles. The **classic style** mainly employs a diagonal stride and the "one-step and double-poling" technique. The **freestyle** requires almost exclusively a skating motion and double-poling technique.

CATEGORIES OF SKIS

The skis commonly called **classic skis** are intended for the classic style; those specially designed for the freestyle are known as **skating skis.** Some manufacturers have developed **combi skis,** which allow you to do both the classic style and the freestyle. You must wax them according to the style of skiing desired. There are, however, fewer and fewer combi skis on the market.

Off-trail skis are designed to enable the skier to move about more freely off trails. They are sturdier, wider, and have metal edges. They must be waxed like classic skis.

Telemark is a turning a technique used only for going downhill. **Telemark skis** have cambers designed specifically for this purpose and hence they cannot be used for the classic or freestyle. Their metal edges and cambers are similar to those on downhill skis, and they are waxed like skating or downhill skis.

TYPES OF SKI BASES

Synthetic bases

A Swiss firm, Inter Montana Sport (IMS), was the first to manufacture and distribute **polyethylene** (also called **P-Tex**) for ski bases. Several other companies now market polyethylene products under different names, but P-Tex is the term most commonly used. There are two types of P-Tex.

Sintered P-Tex is made from polyethylene powder that is heated and pressed into blocks. The blocks are then cut to form bases of the desired width, length, and thickness. New technologies also have made it possible to produce sintered P-Tex, namely DuraSurf 2001, directly to the desired measurements without any cutting. Sintered P-Tex has a high molecular weight, which gives the base very high wax absorption capability, excellent shock and scratch resistance, a low friction coefficient, and better gliding capability.

Sintered P-Tex can be either black or transparent. Black P-Tex, sometimes called "Electra," contains between 10 and 20 percent graphite, which increases its thermal and electrical conductivity and helps reduce the amount of water between the base and the snow. Moreover, pollutants and dirt in the snow do not seep through to a black P-Tex base as readily. Black P-Tex, however, is less scratch and shock resistant than transparent P-Tex, and it is generally used at lower temperatures. At higher temperatures, skiers usually opt for skis with transparent P-Tex bases.

Sintered P-Tex is a high-quality product used especially in the manufacture of top-of-the-line skis.

Extruded P-Tex is also made from polyethylene powder, but the powder is heated and molded to the desired dimensions. Because it has a lower molecular weight, extruded P-Tex does not perform nearly as well as sintered P-Tex. It absorbs wax to a lesser degree and offers less shock resistance. Extruded P-Tex is generally used in the manufacture of lower- and average-quality skis.

Another type of synthetic base is made of **acrylonitrile butadiene styrene** or **ABS**. These are poor quality bases that cannot be heated with a waxing iron. They do little for performance and cannot absorb wax.

Wooden bases

Wooden bases retain wax quite well. The varieties of wood may vary, but they all possess the same properties with respect to waxing. In general, wooden bases provide an average performance that suits many skiers.

TYPES OF WAXES

Grip wax

Grip waxes enable skis to stick to, grip, and glide on snow, depending mainly on the snow granulation and the temperature. They are applied to the bases of classic skis only. Grip waxes are sold in jars, tubes (klister only), and aerosol sprays.

Some grip waxes are made up of hydrocarbons. These waxes are manufactured from petroleum derivatives and sometimes contain tar. They are inexpensive and well suited to novice and intermediate skiers.

WAX COMPOSITION

Waxes are made of natural or synthetic products that affect ski performance in specific ways. Wax manufacturers conduct extensive research, testing their products on trails in Europe, Asia, and North America. Once they have optimized the performance of the waxes they market, manufacturers keep their wax composition formulas a secret.

NATURAL INGREDIENTS

Beeswax	Improves glide
Paraffin wax	Improves glide
Pine tar	Improves grip and glide
Resin	Improves grip

SYNTHETIC INGREDIENTS

Hydrocarbons	Improve grip and glide
Fluorocarbons	Improve glide
Teflon	Improves glide
Graphite	Improves glide at very low temperatures
Silicone	Improves glide at relatively high temperatures
Hardener	Improves glide at very low temperatures
Silver	Prevents snow residue from soaking into klister
Coloring	Makes it possible to differentiate waxes

In recent years, lubricants containing fluorocarbons occasionally have been added to grip wax to improve gliding and boost resistance to snow contaminants and water. Fluorocarbon waxes, as they are known, may have low or high fluorocarbon content. They are very expensive and effective, and are intended mainly for advanced skiers.

Grip waxes are distinguished by their makeup and hardness. They come in a variety of colors, each corresponding to an outside temperature range, snow granulation, and humidity level. Although every wax manufacturer has its own wax color system, in general the most commonly used waxes are green, blue, purple, red, and yellow, used in temperatures ranging from coldest to warmest.

When the name of a wax is modified by "special," "extra," or "super" (depending on the manufacturer), it means that the wax must be used at a temperature warmer or colder than the one recommended for the regular color wax.

There are some universal waxes that cover a broad range of temperatures and are used most often by novice skiers. There are two types: one for dry snow and one for wet snow.

Glider wax

Glider waxes allow for continuous and prolonged glides in the snow depending on temperature, snow granulation, and humidity levels. They can be used on the bases of both classic and skating skis. Glider waxes are sold in stick, block, powder, liquid, paste, aerosol spray, and granular forms.

Like grip waxes, glider waxes are made up of hydrocarbons or fluorocarbons. The ones containing fluorocarbons may have low, high, or 100 percent fluorine concentration, and some also contain graphite. Fluorocarbon glider waxes are more expensive, more effective, and are best suited for advanced skiers.

Glider waxes, too, come in a variety of hardnesses and colors, including a universal style that is effective in a broad range of temperatures.

Additive wax

Additive waxes, used alone or mixed with glider waxes, enhance a ski's glide. They are made of silicone, hardener, and graphite, and are sold in stick, block, and powder form. Some glider waxes are sold with additives premixed.

Binder wax

Binder wax is a resinous, very sticky substance used only on classic skis to bind the wax of the day to the ski base. Binder wax not only makes it easier to apply the grip wax, it also helps the grip wax to stay on the base longer, especially in coarse snow. It is sold in jars, tubes, and aerosol sprays.

DETERMINING THE GRIP ZONE

For classic skis, it is important to determine the grip zone, or waxing pocket, accurately. To do so, place the skis flat on the floor and slide a sheet of stiff paper under a ski. Step into the bindings and spread your weight evenly on both skis. Have someone move the sheet of paper from front to back under the binding. The area where the paper can slide is the waxing pocket. This is where binder wax and/or the grip wax of the day is applied.

The length of the pocket is affected by certain variables.

- A stiff camber requires a longer pocket.
- A long ski requires a longer pocket.
- A heavier skier needs a longer pocket.
- An advanced skier may opt for a shorter pocket to lengthen the glide zones and increase gliding capability.
- In general, the warmer the temperature outdoors, the shorter the pocket should be.
- If a klister is used, the pocket must be shorter.

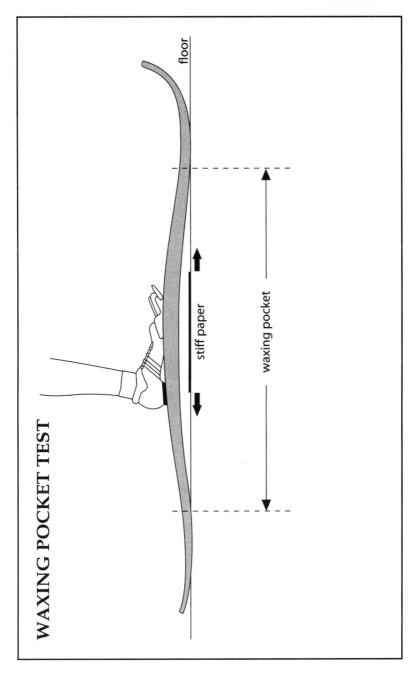

WAXING POCKET TEST

floor

stiff paper

waxing pocket

WAXING ZONES

Depending on the skiing style, the type of base, and the skier's skill level, a ski base might have a single waxing zone or be divided into three or even five zones. A ski with one waxing zone is waxed with either grip or glider wax from tip to tail. In contrast, a ski with three or five zones uses a combination of grip *and* glider waxes.

One waxing zone

A grip zone that extends along the entire base is a good choice for novice skiers using classic skis (synthetic or wooden) and for skiers using off-trail skis. A glide zone that covers the entire base is appropriate for freestyle or telemark skiers.

Three waxing zones

The three-zone waxing technique is used exclusively on classic style skis. The skis have glide zones at the front and back, and a grip zone in the middle.

The grip zone extends from the back of the heel plate to 12 to 18 inches (33 to 46 cm) in front of the binding. The exact length depends on the camber, the length of the ski, the skier's technique and arm strength, the level of difficulty and condition of the trail, and the snow granulation. The stiffer the camber, the longer the grip zone and the shorter the glide zones. Longer skis have longer grip and glide zones.

Optimal ski performance depends on the grip wax, since the goal is to obtain the best possible adhesion using a short grip zone. A short grip zone results in better gliding action.

Five waxing zones

Dividing ski bases into five distinct waxing zones is useful especially for intermediate skiers who practice the classic style under changing snow conditions. There are three grip zones—central zone flanked by two intermediate zones—and glide zones at the front and back.

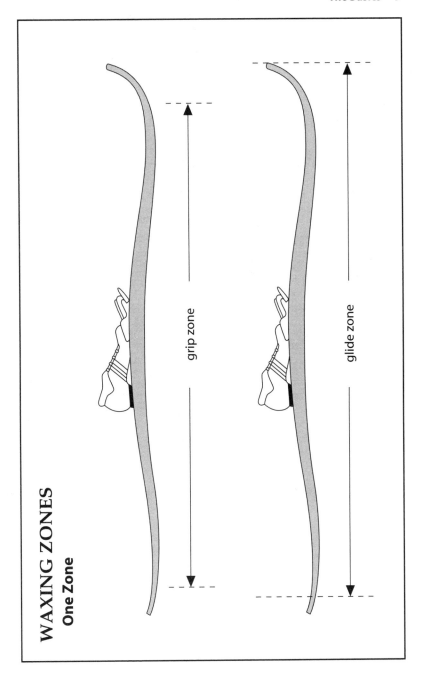

WAXING ZONES
One Zone

grip zone

glide zone

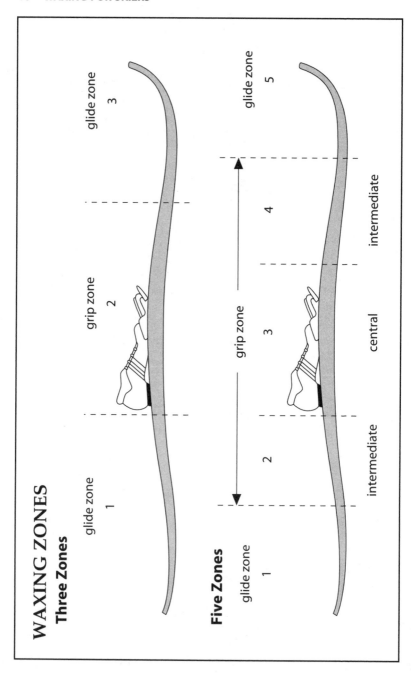

WAXING ZONES
Three Zones

glide zone 1

grip zone 2

glide zone 3

Five Zones

glide zone 1

intermediate

grip zone

intermediate 2

central 3

intermediate 4

glide zone 5

The front intermediate zone is longer than the rear intermediate zone. It extends from 7 to 11 inches (20 to 30 cm) behind the heel plate to 12 to 19 inches (33 to 50 cm) in front of the binding, depending on the camber, the length of the ski, the skier's technique and arm strength, the level of difficulty and condition of the trail, and the snow granulation.

The central grip zone extends from in front of the binding to the heel plate.

APPLYING THE WAX

Waxes should be applied to prepared skis in a specific order.

On synthetic classic skis, apply binder wax first (if you choose to use it), then grip wax, to the grip zones. Apply glider wax (if you choose to use it) directly to the base in the glide zones. Some skiers save time by foregoing the layer of binder wax in the grip zone or by omitting the glider wax entirely.

When using synthetic skis for freestyle skiing, apply glider wax to the entire length of the ski.

Spread a coat of pine tar on the entire length of wooden skis, followed by a layer of binder wax and a layer of grip wax from tip to tail. To save time, some skiers skip the binder wax; the grip wax, however, will last longer if binder wax is used.

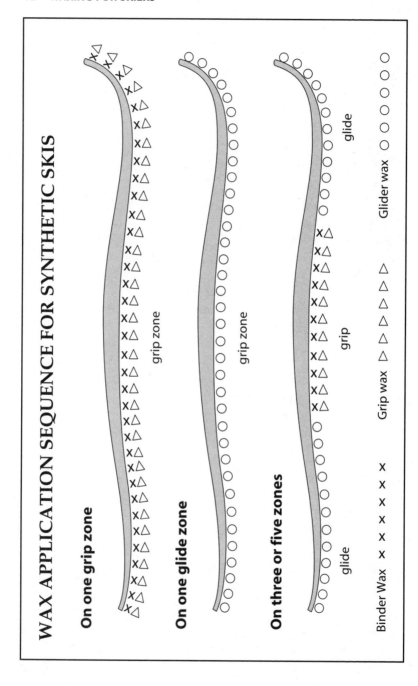

WAX APPLICATION SEQUENCE FOR SYNTHETIC SKIS

On one grip zone

grip zone

On one glide zone

grip zone

On three or five zones

glide

grip

glide

Binder Wax x x x x x

Grip wax △ △ △ △ △

Glider wax ○ ○ ○ ○ ○

2

Synthetic Skis

SKI PREPARATION
Preparing the ski means leveling and smoothing out the base, a
process that is the same for both classic and skating skis.

New skis
When skis leave the factory, the bases are sometimes bumpy,
deformed, or uneven. It is important to correct these flaws before
you wax.

Beginning and intermediate skiers
When sanding, you must use glass, aluminum oxide, or silicon carbide sandpaper. For a smooth sanding surface, wrap the sandpaper
around a sanding block, a plastic scraper, or a synthetic cork (*see
photos 1 and 2*).

1. Sand the entire base using first 220- and then 320-grit sandpaper, or use only the latter until the base is smooth and even (*see
photo 3*). Allow about five minutes per ski.

2. After sanding, work the base from tip to tail with a nylon
brush (*see photo 4*).

Photo 1

Photo 2

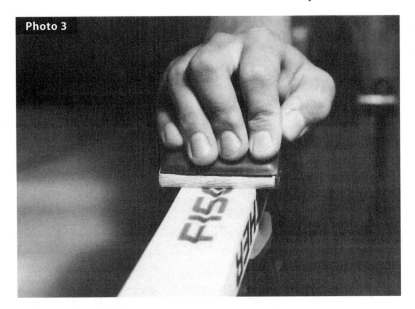

Photo 3

3. Clean the base with a synthetic cloth (*see photo 5*). At this point, the base is ready to be waxed.

Advanced skiers

1. Sand the entire base from tip to tail using 180-, 220-, and then 320-grit sandpaper. Sanding takes about ten minutes per ski.

2. Work the base with a nylon brush and a silicon carbide pad to remove all residue (*see photo 6*).

3. Clean the base with a synthetic cloth and allow five minutes to dry. The base is now ready to be waxed and structured.

Remarks

- Instead of sanding, you can scrape the base carefully from the tip to the heel with a metal scraper or one with a built-in razor blade until the surface is smooth and even. Brush with a silicon carbide pad.
- You can clean the sanded base by spreading a glider wax with a hot iron. Scrape away the excess wax while it is still hot.

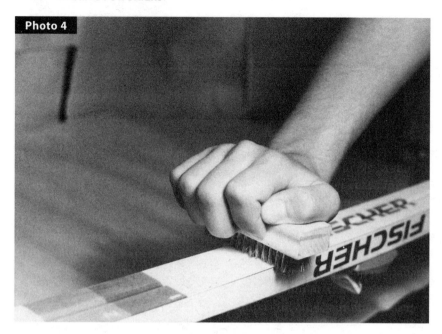

Photo 4

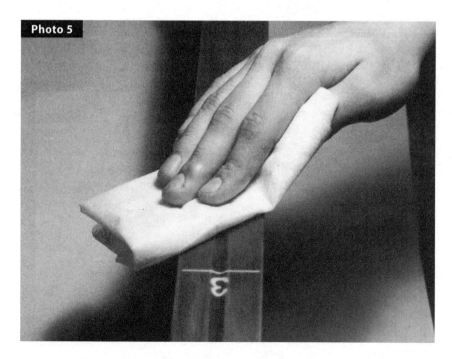

Photo 5

Photo 6

Used skis

When your skis become slower because the bases are uneven, grooved, damaged, or dried out, you may have to smooth the surfaces using the same procedure outlined for new skis. Before sanding, however, you must thoroughly clean the skis according to the method described in the Cleaning the Base section on page 35.

Advanced skiers can prepare old bases with a stone grinding machine using the procedure for structuring described on page 28.

APPLYING BINDER WAX

Binder wax is used mainly for very rough snow and for long outings or ski marathons. It is applied only to the grip zone of synthetic classic skis. Depending on the kind of grip wax you use, there are several binder wax options.

Photo 7

Hard binder wax under grip wax

1. Apply hard binder wax directly to a hot electric waxing iron (*see photo 7*), then carefully spread the hot wax on the grip zone.

2. Smooth the wax with the hot iron, making sure that the base is covered with a thin, even coat (*see photo 8*).

3. Use a plastic scraper and a synthetic rag to remove excess wax from the groove and sides of the ski.

4. Press hard with a synthetic cork to even and smooth the base (*see photo 9*).

5. Allow to cool for ten to fifteen minutes.

Remarks

- A variation is to spread the binder wax on the grip zone, even it out with a hot iron, and allow it to cool. Scrape off the excess and smooth out with a synthetic cork.

- Hard binder wax can be stored in the freezer, which makes it easier to apply.

Photo 8

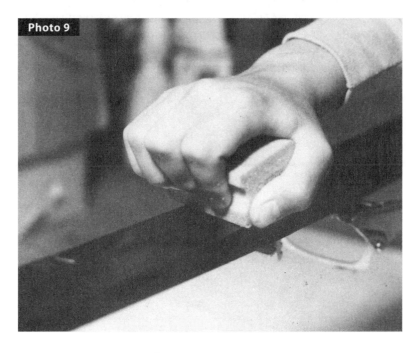

Photo 9

- You can apply two very thin coats of grip wax to the binder wax. This will avoid mixing the grip wax of the day with the binder wax, which also ensures that the latter will last longer. The first coat of grip wax must be heated gently and smoothed out, and the second coat smoothed out only.
- Some skiers use a klister as a binder wax for the hard grip wax of the day.

Aerosol binder wax under hard grip wax

Aerosol binder wax is frequently used on synthetic skis because you can apply a thin coat quickly.

1. Spray the binder wax onto the grip zone and spread it out with your fingers.

2. Use a hot iron to work the wax into the base.

3. Smooth out wax with a synthetic cork and allow to dry for five minutes before smoothing again.

Hard grip wax of the day as a binder wax

Some skiers do not use any specific binder wax, applying instead an additional layer of the hard grip wax of the day.

1. Apply a layer of grip wax of the day.

2. Go over it with a hot iron for a thin, even coat.

3. Smooth wax with a synthetic cork.

4. Allow to cool before applying the other grip waxes of the day.

Klisters

You can use a blue or green klister or Chola by Rode as a binder wax for daily klisters. Apply the blue or green klister and allow it to cool for ten to fifteen minutes outside before applying the klister of the day. Alternatively, you can simply apply two coats of the klister of the day; the first coat replaces the binder wax. You can heat the klister in a small container and spread it with a paint brush. This is also a very effective way of mixing various klisters (*see photo 10*).

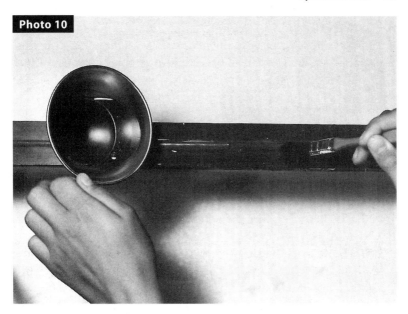

Photo 10

Photo 11

APPLYING GRIP WAX

Grip wax is applied only to the grip zone of synthetic classic skis. Immediately after preparing the ski or after spreading the binder wax on the grip zone, apply the hard grip wax or the klister of the day.

Hard grip wax

1. Apply a thin, uniform coat of wax on the base and in the groove of the grip zone (*see photo 11*).

2. Smooth and polish with a synthetic cork to obtain a transparent layer of wax.

3. For better performance, repeat steps 1 and 2 several times.

Remarks

• The first coat of grip wax can be heated with a hot iron before a second coat is applied. The grip wax will last longer this way, and it will also act as a binder wax.

• The last coat of grip wax can be evened out with a hot iron. This also helps to bind the wax to the other coats.

Photo 12

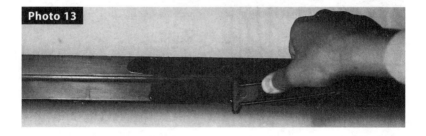

Photo 13

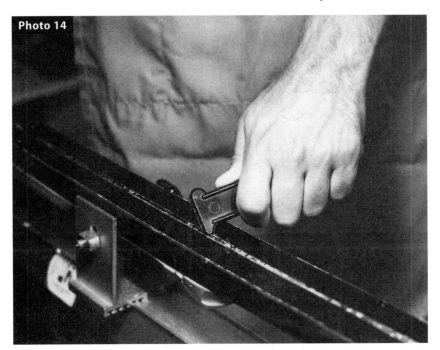

Photo 14

Klisters

1. Apply the tip of the tube directly to the base and spread a thin coat of wax on each side of the groove (*see photo 12*).

2. Spread klister evenly using the small applicator provided with each tube (*see photo 13*).

3. Use the corner of a plastic scraper or a klister applicator to remove excess wax from the groove and the sides of the ski (*see photo 14*).

4. Allow the wax to cool outside for five to ten minutes before skiing.

Remarks

• Klister in the tube is preferable to aerosol klister because it stays on the base longer and is less expensive. Aerosol klister can save time, though; just spray it on, spread evenly, and allow to cool.

STRUCTURING THE BASE

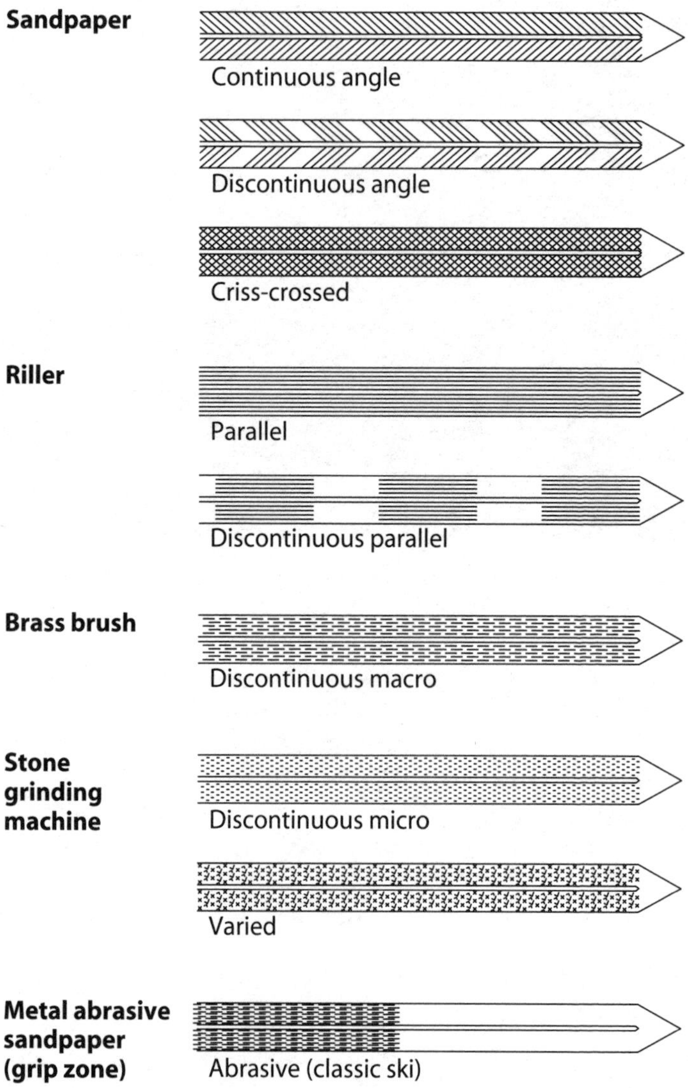

Sandpaper

Continuous angle

Discontinuous angle

Criss-crossed

Riller

Parallel

Discontinuous parallel

Brass brush

Discontinuous macro

Stone grinding machine

Discontinuous micro

Varied

Metal abrasive sandpaper (grip zone)

Abrasive (classic ski)

- If the wax is too hard, you can warm up a tube of klister with your hands, a match, a lighter, or a hand-held torch, or by placing it in hot water. It will then be easier to apply.
- Used tubes of klister may leak. Store them in small plastic bags to avoid soiling your waxing kit.
- Remove klister from skis before storing them indoors; heat may cause the klister to run down onto the floor.

STRUCTURING THE BASE

Structuring means creating shallow parallel grooves of varying widths or somewhat deeper and more regular patterns in the base. Structures improve gliding by reducing tension between the base and the snow, thereby lessening friction. They also break down water molecules further, which reduces suction.

Glide zones are structured after the base has been prepared and before glider wax is applied. This procedure is intended for advanced skiers only, and there are several methods.

Sanding

1. Sand the glide zone(s) lengthwise along one side of the groove then the other, for about five minutes per ski.

Choose the correct sandpaper based on the outdoor temperature.	
32° F and above (0° C and above)	80-grit
27° to 31° F (-1° to -8° C)	180-grit
5° to 27° F (-8° to -15° C)	220-grit
5° F and below (-15° C and below)	320-grit

2. Brush the base with a silicon carbide pad to eliminate residue.

Remarks

- This is the most commonly used method of structuring the base.
- The base on both sides of the groove can also be sanded at an angle. Changing the sanding angle creates different types of structures.

Structuring with a riller

Choose the right file based on the outdoor temperature.

32° F and above (0° C and above)	1 mm (rough)
17° to 31° F (-1° C to -8° C)	.75 mm (medium)
16° F and below (-9° C and below)	.5 mm (fine)

1. Press hard on the riller and work in a tip-to-tail direction on the glide zones to create parallel grooves (*see photo 15*).

2. Level the grooves with a metal or bladed scraper.

3. Brush the base with a silicon carbide pad to soften the top part of the grooves.

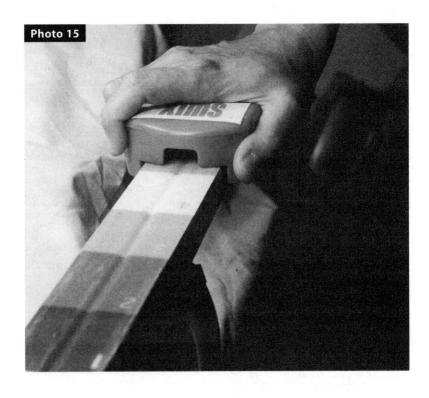

Photo 15

Photo 16

Remarks
- This method produces straight and fairly rough grooves that channel water effectively.

Structuring with a brass brush

1. Brush the glide zones firmly and constantly with a brass brush (*see photo 16*).

2. Brush the base again with a silicon carbide pad to remove residue.

Remarks
- This method, which creates patterns of varying depths in the base, is especially useful for skiing on wet snow in temperatures above freezing.
- Instead of a brass brush, you can use a metal scraper, which creates fine, uneven, and shallow structures. This method is most effective for cold snow and is intended for advanced skiers.

Structuring with a stone grinding machine

1. Set the machine, adjust the stone, and run the glide zones of the ski over the stone several times.

2. Use a metal or bladed scraper to even the grooves. Remove residue on the base with a silicon carbide pad.

Remarks

- A stone grinding machine designed to tune up downhill skis can also be used to structure cross-country skis.
- A host of patterns can be created by adjusting the setting of the grinder. The structure of the stone, its rotations per minute, the diamond dressing speed, the pressure applied to the ski, and the speed at which the ski is run through are major factors in creating the desired structure.
- Structures can be shallow, parallel, pointy, spaced out, rough, even, discontinuous, short, long, or angled. In general, fine, compacted, and parallel structuring is well suited to cold temperatures, whereas rough, spaced out, and angled structuring is preferred when temperatures are warmer.
- In specialized shops, skilled technicians use stone grinding machines to structure skis.

You should proceed with caution when performing this delicate operation to avoid damaging the base of the ski. Cross-country skis have thinner bases than downhill skis, and they cannot be structured as deeply or as often.

Structuring for a waxless ski effect

Waxed synthetic classic skis can be altered so that they can be used as waxless skis.

1. Establish a grip zone of about 15 inches (40 cm).

2. Using a sanding block and 50- or 160-grit metal abrasive sandpaper sand the length of the grip zone firmly.

3. Keep sanding vigorously until small grooves and polyethylene strands appear.

4. Apply liquid silicone to the sanded surface and allow to dry.

Remarks

This technique can be used on only some bases, such as sintered polyethylene bases. Avoid using on extruded polyethylene bases.

APPLYING THE GLIDER WAX
Synthetic Skis

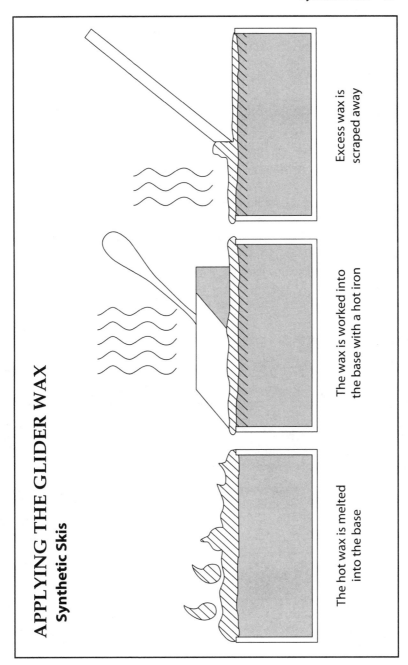

The hot wax is melted into the base

The wax is worked into the base with a hot iron

Excess wax is scraped away

To restore the base to its original state, repeat the same steps required to prepare a new ski.

APPLYING GLIDER WAX

When the base has been prepared and/or structured, you can apply glider wax to the glide zones of classic or skating skis. The method of application varies depending on the type of wax used.

Hard glider wax (with or without fluorocarbons)

1. Heat the glider wax of the day with an electric waxing iron (*see photo 17*) and allow the wax to drip on the glide zone(s), creating two thin trails of wax, one on either side of the groove.

2. Run the iron over the base several times to even out the surface and achieve penetration. The longer you spend ironing the base, the more it will absorb the wax. Allow at least five minutes per ski for the wax to penetrate.

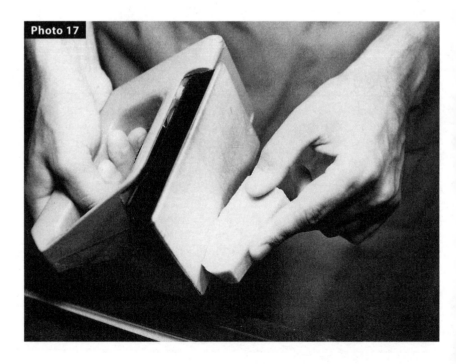
Photo 17

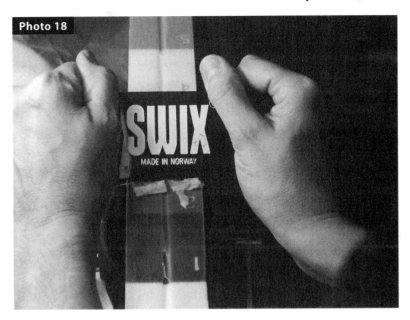

3. Allow the wax to cool completely.

4. Use a plastic scraper to remove as much of the wax as possible. Do not scrape too hard, as that could modify the structure of the base (*see photo 18*).

5. Brush the base with a nylon brush until the fine wax particles disappear from the surface.

6. Polish with a horsehair brush and a polishing block (*see photo 19*).

Remarks

- If smoke appears while you are heating the wax, your iron is too hot. You run the risk of altering the properties of the wax and damaging the base, and toxic gases may be produced.
- Glider waxes of the day (without fluorocarbons) can be used as the first glider wax before the 100 percent fluorocarbon glider waxes of the day are applied.
- Some advanced skiers apply glider wax to the sides of the ski to improve their gliding capability. Use a universal liquid or paste glider wax. Spread the wax and allow it to dry. Polish with a soft cloth.
- Glider wax containing graphite can be used on sintered black polyethylene bases. Those bases, which are made with graphite, are prepared and structured in the same way as sintered transparent polyethylene bases.

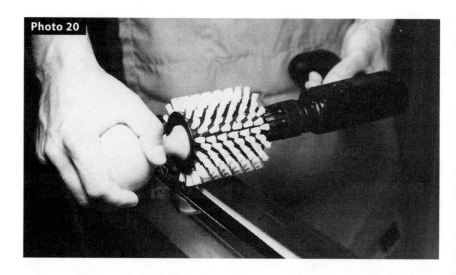

Photo 20

Quick Method

In warmer temperatures, you can rub glider waxes directly on the base instead of using the drip method. Glider waxes can be softened slightly with a hot iron and rubbed on the base in colder temperatures.

Instead of brushing the base manually, use a drill-powered roto brush (*see photo 20*).

Paste or liquid glider wax

These are effective glider waxes well suited to beginners or people in a hurry.

1. Spread the wax evenly on the base with the cloth provided.
2. Allow to dry for about two minutes.
3. Rub with a horsehair brush or polish with a synthetic cloth.

Remarks

- These waxes are handy for quick applications while out on the trail.
- Apply paste and liquid waxes to the tops of skis to prevent snow from sticking, and to the sides of skis to improve gliding.

Powdered 100 percent fluorocarbon glider wax

Prepare and structure the skis, apply the glider wax of the day—preferably one with low or high fluorocarbon content—and then apply the powdered 100 percent fluorocarbon wax.

PRECAUTIONS

Some waxes or additives used in very cold temperatures crumble when they are cold-scraped. It is recommended that you wear goggles. It is preferable that you remove excess wax while it is still hot and go over it a second time when it has cooled off.

Always wear a mask and work in a well-ventilated area when applying the fluorocarbon wax.

Hot application

1. Sprinkle the wax uniformly on the base on each side of the groove.

2. Spread the powder with a small spatula or a klister applicator.

3. Melt the wax into the base and run over (once if possible) with a waxing iron set at a high temperature (300° F or 150° C) to smooth out the wax. Small sparks appear behind the electric waxing iron when the ideal temperature is reached.

4. Allow the wax to cool for fifteen to twenty minutes.

5. Brush first with a nylon brush, then a horsehair brush, and finish with a polishing block.

Remarks

• One hundred percent fluorocarbon waxes that contain teflon require a higher waxing iron temperature.

Cold application

1. Sprinkle the wax uniformly on the base on each side of the groove.

2. Spread the powder with a small spatula or an oyster knife.

3. Rub the wax hard with a synthetic cork and a nylon brush until a uniform film is formed.

4. Brush with a horsehide brush, a polishing block, or a synthetic cloth until the base shines.

Remarks

• Cold application uses less wax than hot application does.

• Advanced skiers always apply fluorocarbon waxes to the same pair(s) of skis.

Additives

Additive waxes, used alone or mixed with other waxes, increase the gliding capability of skis under specific conditions.

Use an electric waxing iron to heat the additive—by itself or in equal proportion with the glider wax of the day—and apply as you would a hard glider wax.

Glider waxes and additives can also be mixed by heating them in a small container in equal measure. Spread on the base with a synthetic brush.

Remarks

- Some additives can be used as a first layer under the glider wax of the day, particularly if you are using 100 percent fluorocarbon glider wax.

- Additives help to repel snow crystals, resulting in less abrasion on the base.
- Silicone and graphite are the most commonly used additives. Silicone makes it more difficult for water to penetrate through the base and is used in warm temperatures.
- Graphite makes the ski more resistant to abrasion and snow crystals. Additive waxes containing graphite are used only on black sintered polyethylene bases and in cold temperatures. An additive with graphite can be used as the initial glider wax before the glider wax of the day.

CLEANING THE BASE

Ski bases should be cleaned after each outing to remove old coats of wax and contaminants. Clean grip zones first, and then clean the glide zones.

Grip zones

1. Remove as much wax as you can with a plastic scraper. It may help to apply wax remover before scraping.
2. Repeat if necessary.

TRANSFORMING THE BASE

BEFORE   **AFTER**

1. Preparation (used ski)

2. Brushing with silicone carbide (Fibertex)

3. Structuring

4. Applying glider wax

5. Brushing with nylon brush after applying glider wax

3. Wipe the base with a synthetic cloth.

4. Allow five minutes for the wax remover to evaporate.

5. Apply binder wax and/or wax of the day, if necessary.

Glide zones

Follow the steps listed for cleaning grip zones. You may wish to clean the glide zones more thoroughly.

1. Select a glider wax appropriate for temperatures above 32° (0° C). Heat the wax with an electric waxing iron and allow it to drip onto the base.

2. Spread the wax evenly on the base with a waxing iron.

3. Iron nonstop for two or three minutes.

PRECAUTIONS

It is very important that the room where the wax remover is being used be well ventilated.

We advise that you wear a mask to avoid breathing in noxious substances.

It is recommended that persons allergic to wax remover wear gloves.

Dispose of wax remover soaked cloths immediately.

Ensure that the container of wax remover is kept away from any source of intense heat, such as waxing irons and torches.

---

4. While the wax is still hot, scrape it lightly with a plastic scraper. Allow wax to cool and repeat steps 1 through 4 two or three times.

5. Clean with wax remover and wipe with a synthetic cloth. Go over glide zones with a nylon brush.

Remarks

- The tops and sides of skis can be cleaned with wax remover.
- Apply silicone spray or glider wax (paste or liquid) to the tops of the skis to prevent snow from sticking.
- Scented liquid wax remover (aerosol spray or jelly) is available on the market.
- Some skiers do not use wax remover for fear of removing too much glider wax and causing excessive dryness in the base.

REPAIRING THE BASE

Repair P-Tex is available in various forms and colors. Only top-grade, long-lasting P-Tex filaments are as hard as sintered polyethylene bases. Sticks, powder, and strips are used for extruded polyethylene bases.

P-Tex sticks

1. Clean the damaged area with wax remover and allow to dry.

2. Choose a P-Tex stick the same color as the base, and heat it with a torch near the ski base (*see photo 21*). *Note:* Keep the P-Tex stick in the blue part of the torch flame so that the P-Tex does not turn black.

3. Drip enough P-Tex onto the base to cover the damaged area, and allow it to cool for a few minutes.

4. Spread the P-Tex as evenly as possible using a very hot waxing iron.

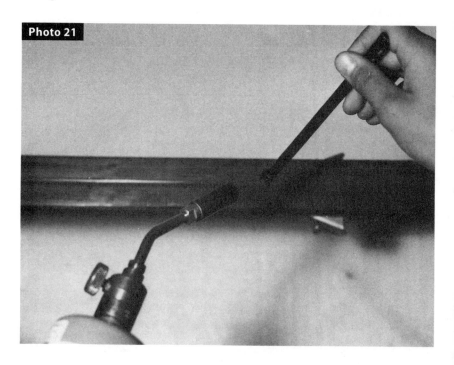

Photo 21

5. Remove excess P-Tex with a metal or bladed scraper.

6. Sand lightly with 320-grit sandpaper.

7. Repeat steps 2, 3, and 4, if necessary, to fill in the affected area completely.

P-Tex powder

1. Clean the damaged area with wax remover and allow to dry.

2. Sprinkle P-Tex powder to fill in the damaged spot (*see photo 22*).

3. Using an electric waxing iron or a hot soldering iron, press and even out the powder. Allow to cool.

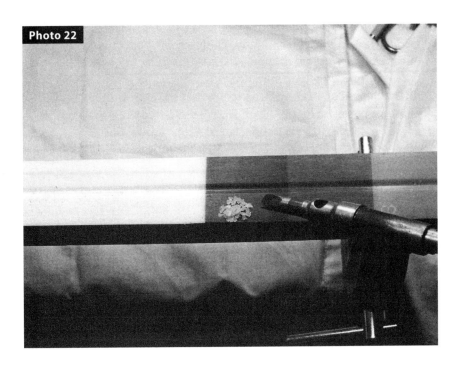

Photo 22

4. Scrape off the excess carefully and smooth the surface with a metal or bladed scraper.

5. Sand lightly with 320-grit sandpaper.

P-Tex strips and guns or irons used to repair P-Tex

1. Use P-Tex strips the same color as the base and avoid overheating the P-Tex.

2. Cover the zone to be repaired and allow to cool.

3. Scrape off the excess carefully and even the surface with a metal or bladed scraper.

4. Sand lightly with 320-grit sandpaper.

Remarks

• Using a gun or iron produces almost perfect repairs in no time. Specialized shops generally use these tools.

WAXLESS SKIS

Waxless synthetic skis are designed with permanent structures in the grip zone. They are well suited for skiers who do not wish to devote much time to waxing. In general, waxless skis have average grip and poor gliding capability. They are most effective when the outside temperature is around 32° F (0° C).

To improve the performance of waxless skis, spray silicone on the structures of the grip zone to prevent snow from sticking. Use liquid or paste waxes on the glide zones and apply them according to the procedure described on page 30 (Applying Glider Wax).

3

Wooden Skis

On a wooden ski, the grip zone runs the full length of the base. There are no specific glide zones as there are on synthetic skis. Waxes, therefore, are applied to the entire base from tip to tail.

The first substance applied is pine tar, which waterproofs the base and keeps the wood from drying out. Next is a middle layer of binder wax. This makes it easier to apply the third layer of grip wax, which in turn lasts longer. Grip wax enables the ski to grip and glide on the snow, depending mainly on snow granulation and outside temperature.

APPLYING PINE TAR

Even if the manufacturer has applied a coat of pine tar to a new pair of wooden skis, it is a good idea to apply another coat.

1. Sand the base with very fine, 320-grit sandpaper, or even it with a metal scraper.

2. Go over the base with a brass brush, apply wax remover, and brush once again.

3. Apply more wax remover and wipe off with a synthetic cloth. Allow to dry.

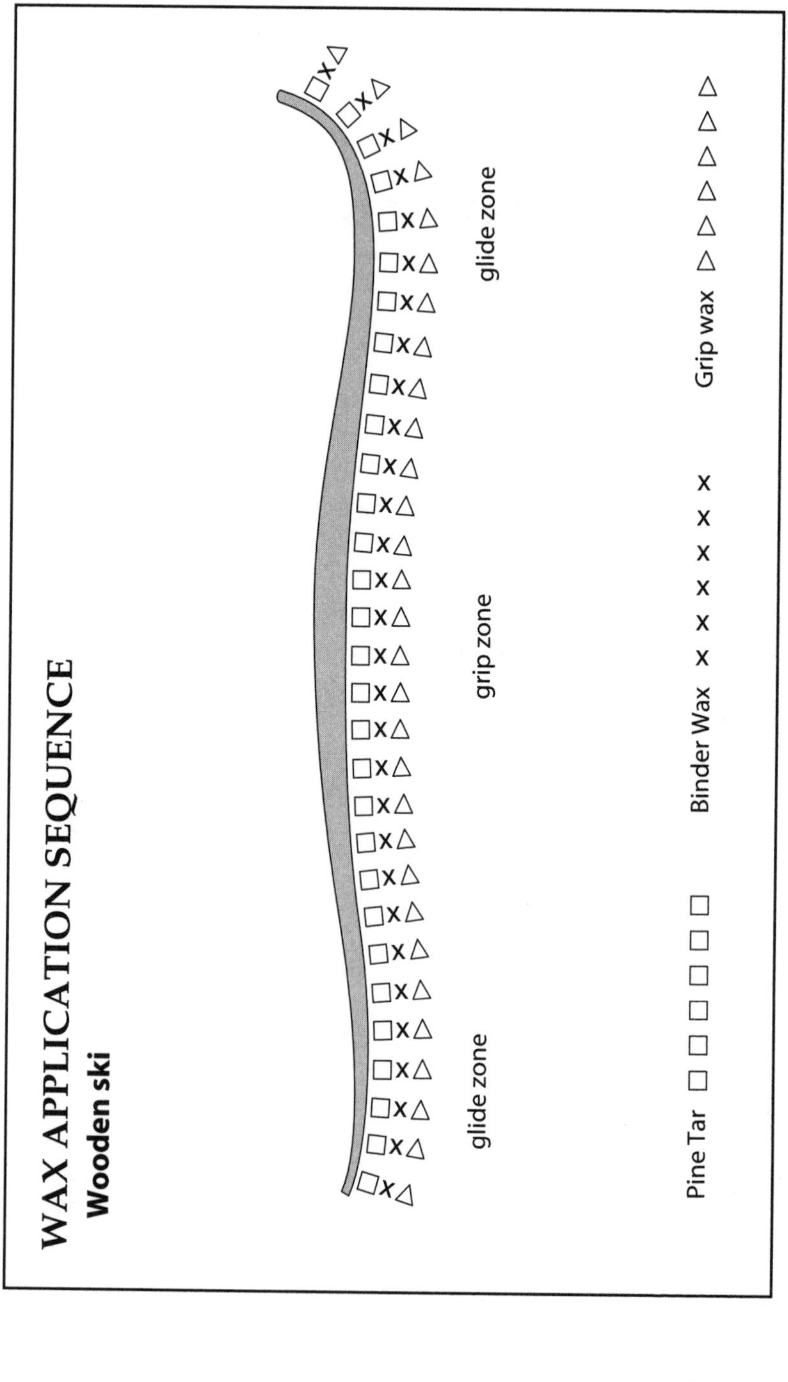

WAX APPLICATION SEQUENCE
Wooden ski

glide zone

grip zone

glide zone

Pine Tar □ □ □ □ □

Binder Wax x x x x x x x x x

Grip wax △ △ △ △ △ △ △ △ △

4. Spread pine tar across the entire base and in the groove (*see photo 23*).

5. Allow to dry inside for at least twenty-four hours.

6. With a torch in one hand and a dry rag in the other, move the torch back and forth over the base, being careful not to burn the surface. Heat the pine tar until small bubbles appear and it turns a brownish color. With the rag, wipe away the excess pine tar where it is still hot (*see photo 24*).

7. Allow the surface to dry fully before applying binder wax.

Remarks

- This application should be repeated where the ski base becomes thinner near the tip and tail.
- Going back and forth over the base with the torch will open the pores of the wood and improve its absorbency.

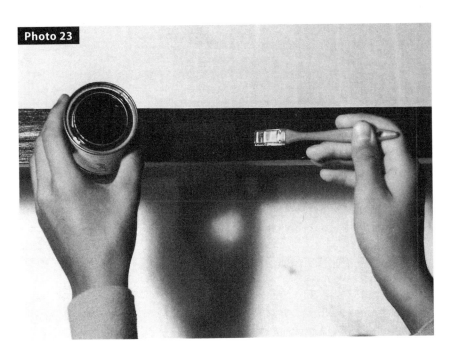

Photo 23

Photo 24

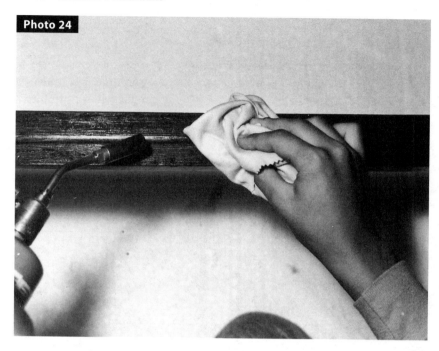

- Repeat steps 4 through 6 to make the skis more waterproof and to ensure greater adherence.

Quick Method

Spread the pine tar without using the torch. Allow it to dry at least four hours inside, then wipe away the excess with a rag.

Pine tar in aerosol containers can be sprayed on the thinner parts of the base. It dries in minutes.

APPLYING BINDER WAX

Hard binder wax

1. Apply the hard binder wax to the surface that has been heated beforehand with a torch (*see photo 25*).

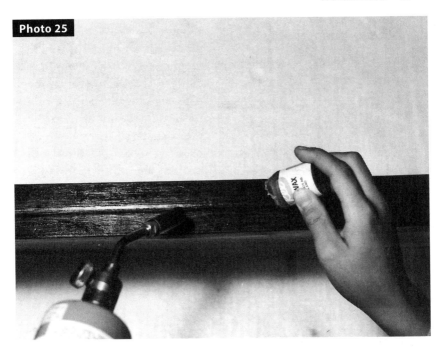

Photo 25

2. With a dry cloth in one hand and a torch in the other, heat the binder wax to a gentle boil. Wipe off the excess with a cloth and repeat this procedure over the entire base.

3. Rub vigorously to smooth out the wax. Allow the skis to dry outside for about thirty minutes.

Remarks

- The hard binder wax can be heated with an electric iron and spread over the base with the hot iron.
- Before applying the grip wax of the day, you can add a very hard grip wax to the binder wax to improve gliding capability.

Quick Method

To shorten the waxing operation, you can skip the binder wax application.

PRECAUTIONS

Handle the torch carefully to avoid burns.

Remember to turn off the torch valve tightly after use.

It is recommended that you wear gloves for the pine tar and binder wax applications.

It is very important that the room in which the tar is being used be well ventilated to avoid allergic reactions or possible poisoning.

Klisters

Apply klister binder waxes to wooden bases as you would to synthetic bases. You can apply a blue or green klister or Chola by Rode as a binder wax for daily klisters. Apply the blue or green klister and allow it to cool for ten to fifteen minutes outside before applying the klister of the day. (Alternatively, you can simply apply two coats of the klister of the day; the first coat replaces the binder wax.)

APPLYING GRIP WAX

Hard grip wax

The procedure is exactly the same as for synthetic skis, except that the grip wax is applied to the entire base.

1. Apply a thin, uniform coat of hard grip wax to the base and groove of the ski.

2. Smooth and polish with a synthetic cork to obtain a transparent layer of wax.

3. For better performance, repeat steps 1 and 2 several times.

Klisters

Klisters are applied to wooden skis as they are to synthetic skis.

1. Apply the tip of the tube directly to the base and spread a thin coat of wax along each side of the groove.

2. Spread klister evenly using the small applicator provided with each tube.

3. Use the corner of a plastic scraper or a klister applicator to remove excess wax from the groove and the sides of the ski.

CLEANING THE BASE

Clean wooden bases as you would the grip zones of synthetic skis, but use a metal scraper instead of a plastic one.

1. Remove as much wax as you can with a metal scraper. It may help to apply wax remover before scraping.
2. Repeat if necessary.
3. Wipe the base with a synthetic cloth.
4. Allow five minutes for the wax remover to evaporate.
5. Apply binder wax and/or the wax of the day, if necessary.

Remarks

- The tops of skis can be coated with marine varnish to prevent the wood from drying out.
- When the base has been roughed up, it can be repaired with Epoxy glue and/or sanded with very fine, 220- to 320-grit sandpaper.

4

Advanced Techniques

The points discussed in this chapter are intended to give you a better understanding of the subtleties of waxing and to help you refine your technique.

HEATING THE BASE

- Heating the base causes the spaces between the polyethylene micro molecules to expand, which allows for deeper wax penetration.
- A regular electric iron can be used to heat and spread the wax, but the surface of the iron must not contain steam holes.
- An electric waxing iron specially designed for waxing is by far the most useful tool. Ideally, opt for a somewhat more expensive iron. They glide better, maintain a con-

PRECAUTIONS

We do not recommend that you heat fluorocarbon glider waxes to temperatures exceeding 570° F (300° C) to avoid burning the waxes completely and producing toxic gas emissions.

stant temperature, and significantly reduce the risk of damaging the base.

- A waxing iron heated by a torch can also be used; however, it does not maintain its heat and is difficult to set to the desired temperature.

- To avoid damaging the base, the iron must be set between 140° and 248° F (60° and 120° C), depending on the hardness of the wax. The iron is set lower for applying soft glider waxes.

- When spreading the wax on the base with a hot iron, keep the iron moving to avoid overheating and burning the base.

SCRAPING

- For scraping the surface of a synthetic ski, use a plastic scraper. Metal scrapers dig more deeply and can alter the structures of the base.

- A ⅛-inch-thick (5 mm) plastic scraper scrapes more deeply than a thin scraper, without digging into the surface.

> ### PRECAUTIONS
>
> **We recommend** that you wear protective goggles when scraping off some glider waxes or additives used for very cold temperatures, because wax particles can rebound from the surface to your eyes.

- Use the corners of a plastic scraper or a klister applicator to remove excess wax lodged in the groove.

- To remove excess wax more easily from the groove and along the edges of a ski, scrape the wax while it is still hot.

SMOOTHING, BRUSHING, AND POLISHING

- The colder it is, the more polished the grip wax must be.
- Always smooth and polish skis lengthwise.
- Synthetic cork is used to smooth and even out the wax; natural cork polishes the grip wax.
- Use three synthetic corks: one for hard grip waxes, one for binder waxes, and one for fluorocarbon waxes.

- A synthetic cloth can be wrapped around a synthetic cork to polish the base.
- Brushing with a silicon carbide pad cleans thoroughly and aligns the P-Tex fibers in the base more effectively.
- Glider waxes containing fluorocarbons must be gone over with a nylon brush and a horsehair brush or a synthetic cork.
- Nylon brushes are good for removing small particles of glider wax between the structures of the base and for cleaning the base thoroughly.
- Brass brushes allow you to structure the base.
- Horsehair brushes or polishing blocks polish the base very effectively and produce a brilliant and gleaming surface.
- A roto brush inserted in an electric drill removes wax particles quickly and effectively. The color, length, and thickness of the brush hairs correspond to those of manual brushes.
- The harder the glider wax, the stiffer the brushes must be.
- Some shops use a machine that spins pressed cloth at high speed to polish the wax and achieve deeper penetration of the base.

LAYERING WAX

The length and thickness of the layers of grip wax depend on many factors: temperature and granulation of the snow; the outdoor temperature; humidity; the type of ski and base; the length and the cambers of the ski; the skier's fitness level and ability; and the length of the run.

Length

- The lower the snow temperature, the longer the grip zone must be. Conversely, the higher the temperature (e.g., above freezing), the shorter the zone.
- There is an exception: When the temperature dips below 5° F (-15° C), the grip zone can be shortened to achieve better gliding capability.

Thickness

- Several thin coats of grip wax are better than one thick coat; when the layer of grip wax is too thick, the ski does not glide as easily.

- The more granular the snow, the more layers of grip wax must be applied.
- When you are planning a long outing, apply one thin coat of grip wax for every 6 miles (10 kilometers). The first coat can be applied with an electric waxing iron.
- If you have two grip waxes and are uncertain about which one to use, you can mix them together by binding them on the base with a hot iron.
- Hard grip wax can be spread on klister, but this technique is intended mainly for advanced skiers.
- If your grip wax does not stick to the base long enough while you are skiing, before your next outing be sure to apply binder wax or try heating the first layer of grip wax with an electric iron.

Hardness

- Softer grip wax should be applied over harder grip wax. If you must reverse the order, a differential of one color is acceptable.
- On synthetic skis, if you decide to create five waxing zones, you must spread softer wax on the central grip zone than on the intermediate grip zones.
- When skiing off trail and/or in very powdery snow, apply softer grip wax (7° to 14° F or 4° to 8° C) and wax a much longer grip zone, possibly even the entire length of the ski. Because the snow is less packed, snow crystals will not penetrate the wax as deeply.
- When skiing in the mountains, remember that the snow is colder at higher altitudes. Apply a harder wax.
- Snow crystals break down more quickly on heavily traveled trails, which means that softer wax must be used.
- To improve ski performance, advanced skiers sometimes apply harder glider waxes on the front part and soft waxes toward the back.

5

Understanding Snow and Wax

SNOW TRANSFORMATION

For cross-country skiing, selecting the appropriate wax of the day depends in part on determining the exact granulation of the snow. To do this, you must understand the snow transformation process.

Freshly fallen snow can be affected by temperature, humidity, wind, sun, rain, trail-grooming machines, ski friction, and many other factors. Snowflakes form with six branches. When the branches become rounded or break, the flakes turn into snow crystals, creating coarse-grained snow. Those nuggets of snow can fuse with others to form wet snow. If the temperature dips below freezing, the wet snow turns into icy snow.

INTERACTION OF WAX AND SNOW

The interaction of snow crystals and ski wax is a very important factor in ski performance. The extent to which they interact depends on the composition and condition of each.

Friction causes snow crystals to penetrate partially the wax on the ski base. This releases energy in the form of heat, which melts the snow to form a thin layer of water that allows the skis to glide.

TRANSFORMATION OF SNOW

Powdered snow
(very dry) - - - - - - - -

Powdered snow
(dry) - - - - - - - -

Dry and hard snow - - - - - - -

Coarse-grained snow - - - - - - -

Wet snow - - - - - -

Crusty snow - - - - - -

Icy snow - - - - - -

INTERACTION OF WAX AND SNOW

Grip phase

Wax is too hard

Wax is too soft

The right wax of the day

Glide phase

The right wax of the day

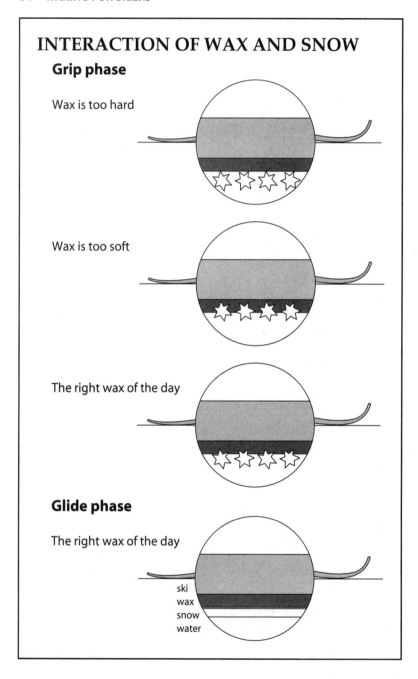

ski
wax
snow
water

Grip wax

For classic skiers, the grip wax acts on the snow in two apparently contradictory ways. It makes the skis adhere to the snow for a better grip, yet it also enables the skis to glide. Selecting a grip wax with the right hardness is crucial to good performance.

If the grip wax of the day is too hard, snow crystals do not penetrate the wax. The skis do not adhere well to the snow but do glide well. If the grip wax is too soft, snow crystals penetrate the wax too deeply. The skis adhere well to the snow but glide poorly. If the grip wax is the right one, snow crystals penetrate the wax to the proper depth, allowing the skis to grip and glide effectively on the snow.

Glider wax

On classic and skating skis, glider wax enables the skis to glide on the snow. Again, choosing the correct hardness is extremely important.

If the glider wax is too hard, the snow crystals do not penetrate the wax and the skis do not glide. If the glider wax is too soft, snow crystals penetrate the wax too deeply and the skis glide with difficulty. If you have chosen the right glider wax of the day, the snow crystals penetrate the wax to the correct depth, allowing the skis to glide freely.

On classic skis, glider and grip waxes interact simultaneously with the snow. Skiers must gain a feel for the wax on the snow to decide whether they have selected the right wax. This comes with experience.

6

Selecting the Waxes of the Day

Before hitting the trails, the classic skier must select the grip wax of the day. Glider wax is optional for a classic skier, but essential for a freestyle skier. Selecting the right wax is important; once you're on the trail, it is too late to change waxes, because hot application is not possible. Wax choices depend on an accurate assessment of current ski conditions and good use of a waxing table.

SNOW GRANULATION

First determine snow granulation at ground level. Pick up a handful of snow in the shade and squeeze it in your glove or mitten.

Dry snow

If the snow falls out of your hand or you cannot make a firm snowball, the snow is considered dry (*see photo 26*).

Photo 26

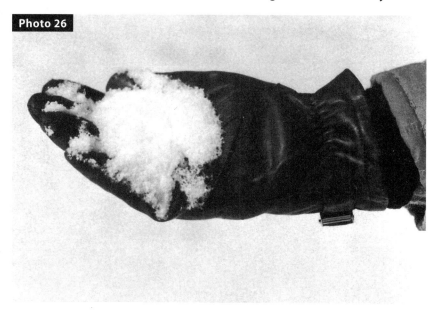

Dry snow is generally encountered when the temperature is below 32° F (0° C). It may be falling or freshly fallen, unmodified, and rough. *Old dry snow* has been on the ground for three or four days. It may be slightly modified or have been packed and changed by the repeated passage of skiers, but it has not thawed or frozen. *Modified dry snow* is severely changed; it is hard, crusty, or icy, and it has either frozen or thawed.

Wet snow

If the snow forms a sticky ball when you squeeze it, it is considered wet (*see photo 27*).

Generally you encounter *wet snow* when the temperature is above 32° F (0° C). Wet snow can be falling or freshly fallen, unmodified, and rough. *Old wet snow* has been on the ground for at least one day. It may be slightly modified. The repeated passage of skiers may have packed and changed the snow, but it has not thawed or frozen. *Modified wet snow* is very wet, severely changed (granular), and has either frozen or thawed.

Photo 27

OUTDOOR TEMPERATURE

The next step in selecting the proper wax is establishing the temperature outdoors. Temperature can vary depending on humidity, altitude, and amount of sunlight. Place an outdoor thermometer in the shade, away from any source of heat, about 4 to 8 inches (10 to 20 cm) above the snow. Allow five minutes for the correct temperature to register. Most wax manufacturers indicate a temperature range on the wax container or in a waxing chart, so you can choose accordingly.

Chemical products are sometimes used to increase the snow's heat resistance. This treated snow, called "chemical snow," remains in snow form even at temperatures several degrees above freezing. Some competition organizers spread artificial snow, which is fresh and dry, along parts of the trails taken by skiers.

HUMIDITY

Normal humidity, under 50 percent, doesn't affect your wax choice. When the humidity is higher, in the 50 to 80 percent range, select a wax that is softer (by 5° F or 3° C) than the one you would use under normal conditions. When humidity rises above 80 percent, or when it is raining, fluorocarbon waxes are the best choice. A hygrometer, which measures humidity in the air, can be a handy tool in a well stocked waxing case.

WAXING TABLES

After determining the snow's dryness or wetness, its granulation, and the outdoor temperature and humidity, consult a waxing table to select the grip and glider waxes of the day. The waxing tables on pages 61 through 75 give an overview of many different brands and waxes, or you can use the tables provided by individual wax manufacturers.

In general, use a hard grip wax on falling or freshly fallen snow. (This type of snow poses the greatest difficulties; fluorocarbon waxes give the best results.) A somewhat softer hard wax is recommended for skiing on old snow. Klister is often the best choice for transformed snow.

TESTING WAXED SKIS ON SNOW

Grip Wax

Once you have selected the grip wax of the day, let the skis cool down outside for at least five minutes before you ski. Cooling completely is especially important when using klisters.

Ski about 1,000 feet (300 m) to check the wax. If the ski slides back when you take a regular diagonal stride on flat terrain or a slight upward incline, try one of the following:
- create a longer grip zone
- apply another thin coat of grip wax
- apply another thin coat of grip wax but do not buff
- use a softer wax
- apply a softer wax but do not buff
- use a klister if you have not already applied one

If the ski does not glide easily during a diagonal stride on flat terrain or a slight downward incline, try the following:
- create a shorter grip zone
- use a harder wax
- use a thinner grip wax

Remarks
- If you have difficulty choosing between two potential waxes, opt first for the harder one. It is easier to apply a soft wax to a hard wax than the reverse.
- The temperature of the snow can be a consideration when you are deciding which wax to use. Snow temperature is generally a few degrees warmer than the air when the outdoor temperature is below freezing; it levels off at 32° F (0° C) when the air temperature moves above freezing.
- Experiment with waxes from one or two different companies.
- Do not overmix waxes.

Glider Wax
- Ski about 1,000 feet (300 m) to check the wax
- If the ski does not glide easily, you can use liquid or paste glider wax to tide you over

7

Waxing Tables

Waxing charts are merely guides; experience will help you make good use of them. For more details, carefully read the instructions on wax containers or in brochures distributed by the manufacturers.

GRIP WAXES
Dry snow (falling or freshly fallen)

Granulation and particularities of snow	Outdoor temperature	REX Finland	RODE Italy	SWIX Norway	START Finland	TOKO Switzerland	VOLA France	HOLMENKOL Germany
Powdered and very cold	3° F and below -15° C and below	Arctic/ Turquoise Mantyranta	Alaska	Polar	Nordic		Polar green	Light green
Powdered and very dry	5 to 18° F -15° to -8° C	Light green	Green special (-22 to 14° F -30 to -10° C)	Green special	Nordic/ Tar minus		Green	Dark green
Powdered and dry	14 to 27° F -10° to -3° C	Green/ Green special	Green	Green/ Green extra	Green/ Tar ten		Blue	Green extra
Dry	23 to 30° F -5 to -1° C	Blue/ Blue extra	Blue/ Multigrade blue special	Blue/ Blue special	Blue Tar five		Blue	Blue
Slightly damp	30 to 32° F -1 to 0°C	Blue special/ Violet special	Super blue/ multigrade violet	Blue extra/ Violet special	Red/Tar two/ Tar zero		Pink	Light blue
UNIVERSAL WAXES	32° F and below 0° C and below	Universal less	Touring less	Lillehammer blue	Universal less	Minus	Mixed base	Universal touring

GRIP WAXES (continued)

Dry snow (old)

Granulation and particularities of snow	Outdoor temperature	REX Finland	RODE Italy	SWIX Norway	START Finland	TOKO Switzerland	VOLA France	HOLMENKOL Germany
Very hard	3° F and below -15° C and below	Turquoise Mantyranta	Green special (-22 to 14° F -30 to -10° C)	Green special	Nordic/ Tar Minus		Green	Light green
Hard	5 to 18° F -15° to -8° C	Green	Green	Green	Green/ Green extra		Blue Tar ten	Green extra
Hard and dry	14 to 30° F -10° to -1° C	Blue	Blue/ Blue special multigrade	Blue/ Blue extra	Blue/ Tar five		Blue	Blue
In transition small grains	30 to 34° F -1 to 1° C	Violet	Violet/ Red extra	Violet/ Special red	Red/ Tar two		Pink/ Yellow	Violet
UNIVERSAL WAXES	32° F and below 0° C and below	Universal and less	Touring less	Lillehammer blue	Universal less		Minus	Universal touring
	32° F and above 0° C and above	Universal plus	Touring plus	Lillehammer red	Universal plus		Plus	Universal touring

GRIP WAXES (continued)
Dry snow (Transformed and cold)

Granulation and particularities of snow	Outdoor temperature	REX Finland	RODE Italy	SWIX Norway	START Finland	TOKO Switzerland	VOLA France	HOLMENKOL Germany
Hard and icy	5 to 18° F -15° to -8° C		Blue klister (skare)	Green klister	Blue klister		Green klister/ Violet klister	Green skare
Hard and crusty	14 to 30° F -10° to -3° C	Blue klister	Blue klister/ special skare/ violet special klister	Blue klister	Blue klister/ violet klister		Blue klister	Blue skare
Transitional coarse-grained and damp	30 to 34° F -1 to 1° C	Violet klister	Violet klister	Violet special klister/ violet klister	Special klister		Violet klister	Violet klister
UNIVERSAL KLISTERS	5 to 18° F -15 to 15° C	OV Tar	Multigrade/ Universal	Lillehammer universal/ Silver universal	Silver tar	Universal		Minus

GRIP WAXES (continued)

Wet snow (falling or freshly fallen)

Granulation and particularities of snow	Outdoor temperature	REX Finland	RODE Italy	SWIX Norway	START Finland	TOKO Switzerland	VOLA France	HOLMENKOL Germany
Transitional	32 to 34° F 0 to 1° C	Violet	Violet/red	Violet extra/ Violet	Yellow/ special Tar zero		Pink	Violet
Damp (forms a snowball)	34 to 37° F 1 to 3° C	Red/ Super red/ Super yellow	Red extra/ Red	Red special/ Red/ Red extra	Yellow/ Tar plus		Pink Yellow	Red
Very wet	37 to 42° F 3 to 6° C	Yellow	Yellow	Pink klister	Red klister/ Tar		Yellow	Red

GRIP WAXES (continued)
Wet snow (old or transformed)

Granulation and particularities of snow	Outdoor temperature	REX Finland	RODE Italy	SWIX Norway	START Finland	TOKO Switzerland	VOLA France	HOLMENKOL Germany
Crusty and damp	32 to 37° F 0 to 3° C	Red klister	Special klister/ silver klister	Violet klister/ Pink klister	Silver klister		Red klister	Red klister/ Silver klister/ Yellow klister
Coarse-grained and very damp	34 to 41° F 1 to 5° C	Ol orange klister/ Brown OV klister	Black nera klister/ Extra klister	Pink klister/ Red klister/ Extra silver klister	Red klister/ Silver klister		Red klister/ Silver klister	Red klister/ Silver klister/ yellow klister
Slush	34 to 60° F 4 to 15° C	Red klister/ OU Yellow klister	Extra klister/ Black nera klister	Red klister	Red klister		Silver klister/ Orange klister	Black klister/ Yellow klister/ Silver klister
UNIVERSAL KLISTERS	5 to 18° F -15 to 15° C	OV Tar	Multigrade/ Universal	Lillehammer universal/ silver universal	Silver tar	Universal		Plus/Minus

FLUOROCARBON GRIP WAXES

Low fluorocarbon hard grip waxes

These waxes are used under conditions of varying snow granulation.

Outdoor temperature	SWIX Norway (Classic)	Outdoor temperature	START Finland	Outdoor temperature	START Finland (with tar)	Outdoor temperature	TOKO Switzerland
19° F and below -7° C and below	Green/Blue	5 to 21° F -15 to -6° C	Green	12 to 16° F -12 to -5° C	Green	-22 to 11° F -30 to -13° C	Green
18 to 30° F -8 to -1° C	Blue	20 to 28° F -7 to -2° C	Blue	19 to 30° F -7 to -1° C	Blue	11 to 29° F -13 to -3° C	Light blue (fresh snow)
30 to 32° F -1 to 0° C	Blue/Violet	27 to 32° F -3 to 0° C	Red	30 to 33° F -2 to 1° C	Red	11 to 29° F -3 to 13° C	Dark blue (old snow)
32 to 36° F 0 to 2° C	Violet/Red	30 to 36° F 1 to 2° C	Violet	14 to 33° F -10 to 1° C	Yellow	28 to 32° F -4 to 0° C	Light red (fresh snow)
34 to 41° F 1 to 5° C	Red/Silver	34 to 37° F 1 to 3° C	Yellow			28 to 32° F -4 to 0° C 32° F and above 0° C and above	Dark red (old snow) Yellow

FLUOROCARBON WAXES (continued)

High fluorocarbon hard grip waxes

Some waxes are used under conditions where snow granulations vary.
For more information, refer to the information appearing on the wax container or in the brochures distributed by Swix.

Outdoor temperature	SWIX Norway X-F	Outdoor temperature	SWIX Norway (X-F)	Outdoor temperature	SWIX Norway (X-F)
3 to 23° F -18 to -5° C	Green	32 to 36° F 0 to 2° C	Silver	30 to 32° F -1 to 0° C	Violet
21 to 30° F -6 to -1° C	Blue	34 to 41° F 2 to 5° C	Yellow	32 to 34° F 0 to 1° C	Red/violet

Low fluorocarbon klisters

These waxes are used under conditions where snow granulations vary.

Outdoor temperature	START Finland	Outdoor temperature	SWIX Norway (Classic)	Outdoor temperature	TOKO Switzerland
27 to 37° F -3 to 2° C	Red	32 to 38° F 0 to 3° C	Red special	-4 to 23° F -20 to -5° C	Violet
34 to 50° F 1 to 10° C	Yellow	37° F and above 2° C and above	Red	5 to 32° F -8 to 0° C	Multirange
		32° F and above 0° C and above	Silver	30 to 32° F -1 to 0° C	Orange
		23 to 50° F -5 to 5° C	Universal klister		

GLIDER WAXES (WITHOUT FLUOROCARBON)

Outdoor temperature	REX Finland	RODE Italy	SWIX Norway	START Finland	TOKO Switzerland	VOLA France	HOLMENKOL Germany	BRIKO Italy
5° F and below -10° C and below	Olive	Light green	Glacier blue	Green	Xcold (powder)	Blue	Red	Antistatico/ Arctic plus/ Cold 9
12 to 21° F -15 to -5° C	Green	Blue	Violet	Blue	Red World Loppet	Blue	Red/Yellow	BK violet 5/ BK red/ Graphite 5
21 to 30° F -5 to -1° C	Blue/Violet/ Light blue	Violet	Pink	Violet/ Red silicon	Yellow World Loppet	Red	Yellow/Graphite	BK yellow
30 to 34° F -1 to 1° C	White/ Yellow	Red/White/ Violet	Pink	Red silicon/ White silicon		Yellow	Yellow	
34 to 40° F 1 to 5° C	Red	Red	Yellow	Yellow		Yellow	Yellow	
36 to 60° F 2 to 15° C	Red	Yellow	Silicon	Yellow		Yellow	Yellow	

GLIDER WAXES (WITHOUT FLUOROCARBON) (continued)

Outdoor temperature	REX Finland	RODE Italy	SWIX Norway	START Finland	TOKO Switzerland	VOLA France	HOLMENKOL Germany	BRIKO Italy
UNIVERSAL WAXES								
32 to 60° F -15 to 0° C	Blue 0° C						Twin	
32 to 60° F 0 to 15° C	Red 0° C					Light green (+silicone)	Twin	
12 to 60° F -15 to 15° C		Universal silver	Nordic Uniglider	Paraffin		Skating (liquid)	Twin	Touring/ QuickSpeedy/ Handy
ADDITIVES					Graphite	Hardener 17/ Arctic hardener	Powerpack GW15 Si	Arctic plus/ Cold 9

GLIDER WAXES (WITH FLUOROCARBON)

Low fluorocarbon content

Outdoor temperature	SWIX Norway	SWIX Norway (graphite)	TOKO Switzerland	HOLMENKOL Germany	BRIKO Italy
5° F and below -10° C and below	Glacier blue	LFG4			Cold 8F
12 to 21° F -15 to -5° C	Violet	LFG6	Nordlite (blue)/ Nordlite + molybdene (graphite)		BK F violet/ BK F red/ BK F red GR
21 to 30° F -5 to -1° C	Pink	LFG8	Premix (Red)		BK F white/ BK F white GR
30 to 34° F -1 to 1° C	Pink	LFG8	Hydro (Green)		BK F yellow
34 to 40° F 1 to 5° C	Yellow				
36 to 60° F 2 to 15° C	Yellow				
UNIVERSAL WAXES					
12 to 60° F -15 to 15° C	Universal F4 (paste)/ Super F4 (paste)/ Superglide 60, 80, 150			Champion EC/ Champion SF	

GLIDER WAXES WITH FLUOROCARBON (continued)

High fluorocarbon content

Outdoor temperature	REX Finland	SWIX Norway	START Finland	TOKO Switzerland	VOLA France	HOLMENKOL Germany	BRIKO Italy
5° F and below -10° C and below	White/ Inari white (powder)	Glacier blue	FC10	Blue Dibloc	Blue		CH florag 6
12 to 21° F -15 to -5° C	White/ Green Lahti (powder)	Violet	FC8/FC820 (powder)	Red Dibloc	Red		CD florag
21 to 30° F -5 to -1° C	Blue	Pink/HFG8 (+graphite)	FC6/FC28 (powder)	Yellow Dibloc	Yellow		DD florag/ Florag 5
30 to 34° F -1 to 1° C	Red/TK140 (powder)	Pink	FC4/FC33 (powder)		Yellow		DC florag5
34 to 40° F 1 to 5° C	Yellow	Yellow	FC2/FC33 (powder)		Yellow		sk4
36 to 60° F 2 to 15° C	TK-72	Yellow	Yellow		Yellow		
UNIVERSAL WAXES 12 to 60° F -15 to 15° C		XF4 (paste)					
ADDITIVES			Graphite (FC12) Hardener (FC20)			Powerpack GW25	

GLIDER WAXES WITH FLUOROCARBON (continued)

100 percent fluorocarbon content

Outdoor temperature	SWIX Norway	TOKO Switzerland	VOLA France	HOLMENKOL Germany	BRIKO Italy
16 to 32° F -5 to 0° C		Streamline (hard or paste form)			
5 to 32° F -15 to 0° C	Cera F Cold (FC 100)				
25 to 60° F -4 to 15° C	Cera F Warm (FC 200)		SP2001	Topspeed PF	HPF1/HPF3

BINDER WAXES

Manufacturers	REX Finland	RODE Italy	START Finland	SWIX Norway	TOKO Switzerland	VOLA France	HOLMENKOL Germany
Hard wax	Orange	Nera	Orange + Orange -	Titan		Orange	Grunvalla
Wax in tubes		Chola					
Wax in aerosol spray cans				Orange			

WAXES AND SPECIAL PRODUCTS

Manufacturer	Products	Description
MAXIGLIDE	Maxx waxx	Universal fluorocarbon glider paste wax
	Sensor Speed	Universal powdered glider wax (also available with graphite)
	XC	Universal liquid glider wax
REX	Micro silicon	Additives for temperatures above 32° F (0° C)
	Rapid Glide	Universal aerosol glider wax
RODE	Universal silver	Wax for all temperatures
	Hand cleaner	Paste cleans hands without water
	Wax remover	Liquid removes wax and cleans bases
SPEED COTE	Wax	Liquid improves gliding capability
	Wax remover	Liquid removes wax and cleans bases
START	Wax remover	Liquid removes wax and cleans bases
SWIX	Crown Spray	Wax prevents snow from sticking to "waxless" ski structures
	Wax remover	Liquid removes wax and cleans bases
	Pine tar	Liquid tar for wooden skis
	Hand cleaner	Paste cleans hands without water
	Chain glide	Dry aerosol lubricant prevents snow from sticking (useful for the tops of skis, bindings, and the soles of cross-country ski boots)
	The Jubilee Waxes	Three waxes with the original colors from 1946. Green: 14° F and below (-10° C). Blue: 14 to 32° F (-10 to 0° C), and Red: 32° F and above (0° C and above)
TOKO	No wax classic	Wax prevents snow from sticking to "waxless" ski structures
	Wax remover	Removes wax and cleans bases (in gel or liquid form)
	P-Tex powder	For repairing the base (transparent or black)
	Dibloc Texwax Nordic	Glider wax in sheets, spread with a Waxmouse (small electric waxing iron)

OTHER WAX AND WAXING ACCESSORY MANUFACTURERS

Conquest
Ex-elit
GRINDrite
Kuusport
SkiGo
SkiVision
Snoli
Vauhti

Dominator
Falline
Hertel
Sandvik
SkiKare
SKS
Solda
Wintersteiger

8

Transporting and Storing Skis

TRANSPORTATION

It's very important to protect the bases of skis while they are being transported.

1. Wax the skis along the entire length. Do not scrape glider waxes.

2. Arrange skis with bases facing each other, and place a piece of synthetic cloth between the ends of the skis.

3. Attach the ends with straps or masking tape.

4. Place the skis in a carrying case.

STORAGE

Before putting your skis away at the end of the season, clean and wax them to prevent them from drying out and to stop oxidation.

1. Clean the skis thoroughly, following the instructions on page 35 for synthetic skis and page 47 for wooden skis.

2. Make any necessary repairs.

3. Sand and even the bases as if you were preparing used skis.

4. Apply pine tar and binder wax to wooden skis.

5. Apply green special grip wax to the grip zone(s) of classic skis.

6. Apply glider wax to the glide zones of skating or classic skis when the temperature is above 32° F (0° C). Do not scrape glider wax.

7. Store the skis in an area where temperature and humidity are stable and at average levels.

Remarks

- When the new skiing season arrives, take wooden skis outside at least two days before your first outing. If the wood has a chance to absorb the humidity, the skis will be less likely to break.

- After every outing, remove the snow that has stuck to wooden skis, especially if they are stored standing up. This will save the skis from cracking.

9

Waxing Cases

Depending on your skill level, you can opt for one of the following assortments of wax and waxing equipment, which you will complete according to your needs.

BEGINNERS
- 220- and 320-grit sandpaper
- sanding block
- nylon brush
- synthetic cloth
- universal hard grip wax for wet snow
- universal hard grip wax for dry snow
- violet hard grip wax
- universal klister
- liquid or paste glider wax
- plastic scraper
- synthetic cork

If you use wooden skis, add the following products:
- metal scraper
- brass brush
- wax remover

- torch
- electric waxing iron
- can of pine tar
- hard binder wax

INTERMEDIATE SKIERS

The intermediate skier's waxing case contains everything in the beginner's waxing case, plus these products:
- sandpaper of various grits
- silicon carbide pad
- roll of synthetic cloths
- several grip waxes (optional)
- several glider waxes

Waxing case, wax remover, torch, klister in tube and aerosol, binder wax in aerosol, plastic scraper, and three grip waxes

- several klisters (optional)
- two synthetic corks
- two ski vises

ADVANCED SKIERS

The advanced skier's waxing case contains these additional items:
- 100 percent fluorocarbon glider waxes
- low or high fluorocarbon glider waxes (optional)
- low or high fluorocarbon grip waxes
- fluorocarbon klisters (optional)
- polishing block
- various brushes

Various plastic and metal scrapers; natural and synthetic corks

Torches, domestic iron, and waxing iron

ADDITIONAL EQUIPMENT

These useful extras can complete a skier's waxing gear:

- electric waxing iron specially designed for waxing
- tool to structure or groove bases
- assorted files
- P-Tex stick or strips for repairs
- apron
- waxing table
- two portable clamps
- cross-country profile
- snow thermometer
- hygrometer

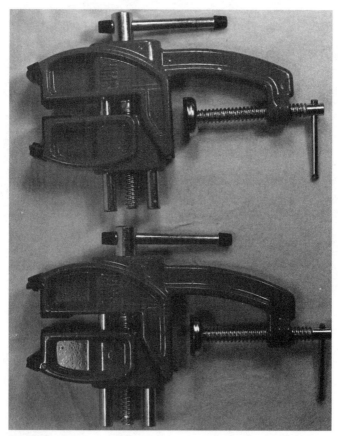

Portable clamps

CONCLUSION

It takes practice and experience to be able to recognize snow granulation, select appropriate wax, and apply it properly. Whether you consider waxing a technique or an art, you can learn to adapt waxing to your needs. This is an ever-evolving discipline; it's up to you to keep up on all the new waxing products, equipment, and techniques. Skiers who take up the challenge, do the research, and experiment continually will enjoy each outing that much more.

All the best with your waxing and may you have many pleasant outings.

Malcolm Corcoran

APPENDIX

WAXING RECORD

Recording certain information about every outing will better enable you to select waxes of the day and to avoid some waxing errors. This sample waxing record can be modified to suit your needs.

SEASON: 1999-2000

Date	Outdoor temperature	Skis	Snow	Structuring	Waxes	Comments
12/20/99	14° F (-10° C)	Classic	Dry	320-grit sandpaper	green	good gliding
1/5/00	28° F (-2° C)	Skating	Falling	Rilled, .75 mm	blue	very fast

TESTING THE CAMBERS OF SKIS

The camber of a ski is the curvature visible between the tip and the tail when the ski is placed flat on the floor. Cambers distribute the skier's weight over the full length of the skis. They are described as stiff, medium, or soft.

It is important to make sure that the camber is suited to the skier's weight. To do so, place the skis flat on the floor and slide a sheet of stiff paper under the binding. Step into the bindings and transfer your weight onto one ski. Ask a helper to slide the sheet of paper from front to back. (*See Waxing Pocket Test illustration, page 7*).

Classic Skis

If the paper does not move, the camber is right.

If the sheet of paper can be moved, the camber is too stiff, making it difficult to flatten the ski to push off correctly when taking a diagonal stride.

Skating Skis

If the sheet of paper moves slightly, the camber is right. If the paper doesn't move, the camber is too soft, and the ski will not glide optimally. The camber of skating skis is longer than that of classic skis.

Remarks

- Factors other than the skier's weight and the skiing style can affect the selection of a ski camber; the skier's technical ability and physical fitness, the wax of the day used, and the condition of the trails can also play a role.
- Advanced skiers may have several pairs of skis with different cambers so that they can adjust better to the various snow or weather conditions.
- A tensiometer is used to measure the tension of the ski camber.

GLOSSARY

Additive. Wax used alone or mixed with glider waxes to enhance gliding capability under certain conditions.

Binder wax. Wax used to adhere grip wax to a synthetic base or to pine tar on a wooden base.

Camber. Curve or arc between the tip and tail of a ski.

Classic style. Cross-country ski style requiring mainly the diagonal stride and the "one-step double-poling" technique. Skis move in parallel tracks.

Combi ski. Synthetic ski used to perform the classic style or freestyle.

Diagonal stride. Ski technique whereby the arms and legs are used alternately in a push-and-glide movement.

Double poling. Cross-country ski technique that mainly consists of a simultaneous backward thrust of both arms while the trunk bends and the legs remain almost straight.

Freestyle. Cross-country ski style in which all cross-country ski techniques can be used freely. Most skiers use the skating technique and double poling.

Glide zone. Area of the ski where most of the gliding action takes place. Depending on the type of ski, this might be the area beneath the tip and tail or the entire length of the ski.

Glide. The capability of the ski to slide easily on the snow.

Glider wax. Wax used to improve glide on snow.

Graphite. Black lubricant mixed with P-Tex in some ski bases and added to certain waxes.

Grip wax. Wax used to push off and glide on the snow. Also called kick wax.

Grip zone. Area of the ski base where the greatest adhesion of the wax to the snow occurs.

Groove. Indentation that runs down the center of the ski base from tip to tail.

Hard wax. Grip wax used generally at lower temperatures, sold in metal jars or plastic containers.

Heel plate. Part of the binding where the heel of the skier's boot rests.

Klister. Grip wax packaged in squeezable metal tubes, used for transformed snow.

Polyethylene. A high- or low-molecular-weight polymer that makes up the bases of most skis and snowboards. A specific brand—and the commonly used synonym for polyethylene—is P-Tex.

P-Tex. A brand of polyethylene.

Riller. Handheld tool used to make grooves in the base.

Silicone carbide pad. Pad or sponge (e.g., Fibertex) consisting of synthetic fibers of various textures. It is mainly used to remove residue from the base of the skis.

Skating ski. Synthetic ski used for freestyle skiing.

Skating. Cross-country technique that incorporates the basic motions of ice skating.

Snow granulation. Variations of snow crystals.

Structures. Modifications to the P-Tex surface of the base that increase glide.

Synthetic base. Base made of synthetic materials of various densities such as polyethylene or acrylonitrile butadiene styrene (ABS).

Synthetic cloth. Very thin synthetic cloth (e.g., Fiberlene) used to clean and polish the bases of skis.

Tail. Rear part of the ski.

Tip. Front curved portion of the ski.

Wax of the day. Grip or glider wax appropriate for the current ski conditions.

Wax. Synthetic or natural product applied to the base of skis to improve the ski's grip and/or glide on snow.

Waxing chart. Table showing various waxes appropriate at particular temperatures and snow granulations.

Waxing pocket. Area where the skier applies the binder wax and/or the grip wax of the day on the grip zone of a classic ski.

Waxless ski. Synthetic ski designed with permanent structures on the base that make waxing unnecessary.

Wooden base. Base consisting solely of wood.